Thoughts In Rhyme

Louis Cecile

Published by Louiville Publishing.

Cover Design by Louis Cecile.

Copyright © 2008 by Louis Cecile.

All rights reserved. No part of this book may be reproduced or transmitted in any form or by any means, electronic or mechanical, including photocopying, recording or by any information storage and retrieval system, without the written permission of the Publisher, except where permitted by law.

ISBN: 978-0-9559900-0-7

December 2008

Dedication

Firstly to my mother for helping me through life
To those who showed me kindness
To the secretaries at primary school who gave me a chance
To Valentina my first love who showed me love
For those who were bad to me
To Zuzia for helping me finish this project
Believe in yourself
Thank God

Louis Cecile
22 December 2008

Given Up

I have a darkness inside
It is a place where I can hide
Into the abyss I wont be missed
People say try I'd rather die
That may seem uncouth
I've been like this since youth
Afraid to face the truth

Have Faith

Do we really want to touch
Can we face the insanity
The rule of thought
The singularity
Price fluctuates with intensity
Tension is beyond normal comprehension
Forever we mention
In life or death recognition
Still the chosen are needed to unleash true humanity
Our survival does not rest with a miracle

Lost Soul

I am lost though not bound
Cannot be found
Floating like a cloud
Into the ether or should that be never
They said I was clever yet where do I be
Come rescue a soul
Search through the forest there be many who hide
Afraid of reality their life begins to slide
Am I back I try to refrain
Lost but found a home in this mist
What type of life I chose it to be this

SMS SOS

I received a text the other day
Asking how I am
I just want to be happy
What's next or should that be new
It feels like I flew in a mist
Now where is my list
That tells me what I knew
My mind is to complex a vortex causing me stress
I try to impress but get left behind with the rest
Wandering lost souls forever we distress
Cannot see light simply no sight
To busy seeing wrong to look for what is right

The Window

Just looking out of the window
As night becomes day
People look up to see my dismay
What can I say what can I do
Day after day wandering what to do
Simply a ghost imaginary host
I need the most
Surviving on toast
Brings me no cheer
Oh please let me not have another year
I wanted so much now left out of touch
Look how young do I be
These four walls are killing
I need two as one is hurting me

Black Birth

You still call me Negro
Can't you think of something new
Your words mean nothing it is life making me a fool
I try till I die at church wondering
All I can do is sigh take drugs or jack a fool
You tell me to learn work 9 to 5 is the rule
Now what have I got I am praying to be shot
I try to survive look at these young innocent lives
If this is all I get birth is a regret

Tears

Cry myself to sleep
I fall so deep
Tears all around
Might deafen the sound
Is it my heart is it my wake
Sometimes in life there is no escape
What is left I can barely draw breath
No need at all pain never crawls
Crying at night tension increases the fight
Violent in thought
I may be caught though already in prison
Confused by light of the perplexing prism

Fake Photo

A beautiful mix to look at your photo
I remain transfixed
You teach divine
Oh love will you be mine
Only you bring joy
Everlasting like time

Early rise

A fawn is not a pawn
It is natural like dawn
It must cower when the beast come to devour
Oh cursed be the morning hour

Rush hour

Bowed so low
My face touches the ground
Do I like to hear the sound of my heart
Beat bringing defeat
How lowly are the weak
God save me
Let me survive another week

Fake Photo 2

Eternal like time
Is this joy divine
Or is it a play that slowly runs out of time
Entertainment none the same
Playing to blame
We are not the same
Though together we are framed

Capitalism

For a moment of existence
A soul to sell
Greed pays bail
My judgment I fail

Please talk to me

It hurts so much
I cannot touch
No one to get nearer
You left because of fear
My enemy it haunts me in the dark
It taunts to create a spark
You embrace its flame and continue the game
I need your touch
I love you so much
You turn away
What happened today
My heart yurns is everything okay

Leave

I walk nocturnal
Even in light
You can see watch out for the darkness in me
Only a few know
They visualize a foul glow
Some can't believe
Oh can it be he
Dare speak my name
You realise fame
Infamously enshrined
I walk till the end of time
What is my crime
A demon I be yet no need to flee
Just let me walk but stay away I can see

Thoughts

I was born with a role
Now what is my goal
Looking inside so deep I can hide
Everything's changed yet still is the same
No one to blame what is the game
It's hurting my brain
Another statistic
Think too much of my life
I now have missed it

Ghetto style

Just heard down my road there has been another killing
And locals call it the thrill of the night
While old folks stay out of sight
I duck and dive to survive
May be paranoid but I stay alive
All I hear is mothers cry
Young kids think their soldiers ready to die
This isn't war but they are making it
Choose your life if you want to make it

What is love

To the earth with no love
I live to bring love
Yet here I remain looking for love
Surely my death will bring me true love?

Which love

Two loves different
Yet they remain indifferent
I can't stand in the way
The way they react ready to attack
Me in the middle now in the back
Torn between the two
What am I to do
Take one side the other calls me a fool
If I sacrifice one what have I become
This situation has left me feeling so numb
I am young and dumb
Chose the wrong one
On the Day of Judgment my punishment will come

Psychosomatic

Twisted contorted inflicted restricted
Inside outside it finds a place to hide
I seek retreat cannot admit defeat
I beg need bread I lay down in bed
The heat feel weak I walk I creak can barely speak
I whisper come nearer my dear feel the fear

Stay strong

We should never harm the heart
Otherwise the world will fall apart

Gender

You want it all yet forget about me
Am I to blame for what has been done
Thy Kingdom comes
Where am I from
Your goal is to see me outdone
Simple in thought is how I am taught
My past has been fought bloody it be
But I am me not he
Now you have no place for me

Excuses

Dear God why...
I use you answer for an alibi

Trouble is coming

Another brother falling
You expect me to be crawling
Too tired to fight on this dark scarlet night
Why waste might
When the flame is about to ignite

Need

From birth we are waiting for touch
It is so loving you want me so much

The Flower

A radiant flower that needs to bloom
Life is cyclical from the womb to the tomb
Receptive to love from above and around
Lay the seeds to nurture the ground
The sound to hear is a blossom awakening
The scent is so captivating
Olfactory note ancient in mind
The noose on the stem can now unwind
Finally set free please can we gather
To look upon this glorious flower

Born Black

The rain forever falls and the black man can scarcely stand tall
For each raindrop is a subconscious tear
The fear of life strikes like a knife, whose holder is either black or white
We are judged, belittled, oppressed, unconsciously beaten till death becomes a golden salvation
Once you open your eyes to the darkness outside, you cry to be blinded again
The left hand of the man controls us like fate, the reason why some us treat the whole world with hate
Others make it and we cannot take, for it seems they have been truly blessed
I stare at the sky and wonder what have I done to deserve this

Winter Flame

Winter Flame brings new essence
Don't leave effervescent
Surround my favourite pronoun enflame
Your tongue releases words showing much pain
Take flight and soar
I love you ever more
The beauty that nurtures free
Future I can see
Spring arrives you seek to depart
Summer's here broken hearts
A winter flame must diminish
Am I duly finished
Winter comes I am frozen
A love so blind my heart is broken

New age women

I want the wo not the man
This role reversal leaves me damned
She don't need me
But I need you
Forget to phone leads to weeks alone
Independent she knows how to set it
My brain is puzzled she has wrecked it
Calls me for a date at eight
Tells me what to have on my plate
No glass of wine a beer is fine
Always she stays on my mind
So complex I can't relax
No need to call her she will fax
Men are simple
One and one is two
I can't figure her out what is there to do
Out with her friends every week till the break of dawn
I call my friends and say I am her pawn
I wonder should I really bitch
When women had to survive men's shit

Wake up

I wake up and see her
Nonchalantly viewing her beauty
I turn to her
Her eyes barely flitter
Failing to meet mine I gaze and sit there
I kiss her lips know warmth truly
Who is the beauty
I can't touch her cheek
For her face is woven
The material is weak
How fooled the adolescent

Boredom

Night and day no sweet song
Life stands still nothing going on
Minutes are hours
Hours are days
What can I do to make it today
Be still my thoughts
Be active I'm caught
Time laughs as it cannot be bought
Eternal master
Brings love
Brings disaster
Bring peace please go faster
Why worry about time it has done no crime
It was me who has been wasting my time

Dream state

I live in a world of dreams
Unseen not been
My thoughts provide a place to hide unseen
From the world become I light
Remain in light the eagle takes flight
I am the world to increase my might
What is real, who can reveal
Confusion decrease my sight
Do I wake up each day or dream in dismay
Are real people walking my way
Totally lost the purpose is done
Life and my dreams are now one

Desperate

It's been centuries
I still can't touch the ceiling
I am stubborn and can't fight the feeling
That beyond the border lays a golden weight
I refuse to listen to colonial fate
Highly educated, highly skilled
It does not matter we still face the same ill
I could easily lay on the floor or look for the exit by the door
If I head for that door I'd really be sore
Cause the ceilings not the high why not try this
If we stand on each others shoulders we must surely reach above it

My brothers

The way some act is a well known fact
That it pushes the rest of us back
I walk down the street
People walk quicker
Now some do see
Others are blind
Some lost their souls
Rotten like swine
Beaten and bruised labelled bad news
No wonder many are confused
Dope, smoke, crack, coke, weed, greed implants new seed
Indeed it's a pit
No need for self pity
This is no way to strive, yes I know it is white city
The trouble I have is that I can't promise much
No fortune, no winning, no instant good luck
Is this our future to be stuck in a rut
Our ancestors cry watching us die
What is the solution
Love, respect in this life and hope for joy in the other
Keep strong to all my poor dear black brothers

Eternal need

The poison I need
Too much will bring greed
Too little brings sorrow
No more equals no tomorrow

Suicide

I live my life in yesterday
The torment brings tomorrow
My sorrow plays a melody
Why I cry
Walk by the river I want to die
Sigh because I am weary
Can anyone hear me
I flee to a new world
A dream a galaxy
It relaxes me and taxes me
What a price to pay
My astral body floats in the bay
My spirit I can't hear it
What have I done
Life is hard when you mentally die young

Living Hell

Trapped in a cell
Inner hell
Wake me up
Ring a bell
This is where I chose to dwell
My mind it can't escape it is the warden
Circular thoughts awake till dawn
Circular thoughts making me their pawn
I yawn from fatigue
Yet still I bleed
I plead with myself
No cheer to good health
You are the controller you are the leader
You are the punisher living in fear
How long can I suffer
How long can I master
I just want to bust the hell out of here
Inner thoughts, personally taught, painfully sought
My mind is circularly caught

The Window 2

Stop and stare at the journey you unwittingly share
The pain in the eyes of the boy who intensely stares
Will the world let him in
Though he shuts himself in
He grins at a couple struggling in the wind
This is nature beginning to end
What does he see
Life passing him by
The realisation brings a tear to the eye
Can he open the window and yell out hi
Tomorrow he will watch more people walking on by

Ghost

When you are dismissed from at an early age
It feels like being put in a cage
No nourishment leads to rot
You dream as child a sleep in the cot
Spirit flies high spirit flies low
Wandering where to go
The whole of me left with no boast
Dismissed I remain a ghost

Acceptance

Infectious smile has infected tears
The laughter strikes with spears
I am not dear and they are not sincere
Feeling fear
I must perform
For when I stop the stage is gone

Unclear

I try
I cry
I remain a little bit shy
I lie to be free
But you eventually see there is something different about me
Fate brings me something to see
Sin of Adam and Eve cannot pacify a paradise to be
Chaotic circle
Circumference keeping us bound
To go on the Merry go
Round and Round
Is this all game
Everything stops when I call out the name

Outsider

Do I have to stay outside
The world is so cold
I no longer feel bold
I keep from thee stories untold
I sit and ponder
While others yonder
Some seek some flee
Others can't survive
All I wanted was a place inside
Is there something wrong
I am human you see
I guess you want to be different
I can see
I look to the left
I look to the right
I look for an entrance whether it takes all night
Finally a sight
A women at hand
I gaze at her beauty as she takes hold of my hand
I solemnly sigh as she leads me to land
I jump to be free
She chases me
Back outside
I am truly free

Constricted

I'm static
I'm static can't move
Not on automatic can't move
My feet are stuck in granite
My brow becomes frantic
I can't stand it
Damn it
Can't run can't move
I'm static
Need help can't move
Need food can't move
Need water can't move
My last breath can move
What life to lose

Light

When you're young
Darkness you rarely see
Light seems to be around thee
When you're old you can see
Reverse the situation what a life to see
The world can't fool you
You've seen the real side
Darkness all around the light comes from inside

Call for help

Abuse is a noose they or you hang yourself with
Words and thoughts
Feelings and emotions cause a commotion
You fall into the ocean
Need devotion
Need divinity
The treasure is not self-pity
In the city you put on a mask to hide the past
But internally you will start to die fast
A cold becomes one
A cold becomes two
Every two months you get the flu
Where is the justice
Where is the hero
If I go on my life will be zero
Yet you are the hero
Seek help to be free
Let someone answer your plea

Water runs free

Spiral into a stream
The barometer of self esteem
Into the whirlpool
Getting lower
The destination is nowhere
Duly sunken
Intoxicated yet not drunken
Let life pass through your eyes
As you gently rise
To your surprise you are free from your prison
To remain afloat you cannot be the unforgiven

Intoxicating

Multicoloured delicious
Turns me from kind to vicious
I cannot escape this artificial high
My eyes hurt and I turn from the sky
A flavour intense
I lose common sense
Dispense my age
Pure fun I engage
Unnatural yet natural effect
I have no regrets a moment of insanity
To skittle down like gravity

Commercial Love

Wake up and smell the roses that make coffers swell
My heart doesn't
A day for the minority
But I am the majority
Full exposure forces me to hide
Oh why should I feel like this
When I can quote statistics to be realistic
This day to realise what I am supposed to miss
People say we pretend by living in this
Once this day is gone
No more love songs
Leading my life today
Single everyday
I can cast that day as another yesterday

Answers

Why am I
The way I am
Do what I do
Does it stem from birth or something in the earth
Is it stars in the sky or due to ancestors that died
Is it due to my gender or if my family were big spenders
Is it because of my town or that I get easily down
Can it be from abuse or lack of affection in my youth
Am I simply in spiral consumed with seeking for the truth
I wonder I wonder
The years don't seem fonder
What can I have missed

Reverse

Going backwards
In the opposite direction
Long from the right path
Cannot see where to go
An alternate reality in reverse
May be a curse
Or does it provide an insight to an overlooked vision

Meaning of life

A meaning of life
The eternal search
Can be seen out the window on a perch
Nature thinks little
The flow of the spirit is simple
A mind not reclined
Is unable to seek divine
Selfish without self
Disturbs our health
Often mistaken as a cure our need for wealth
Forever seeking
External our need
Internal love is what we need to receive

Believe in Love

The twinkle not in the sky
A look that passes on by
A lift when love starts to drift
No myth when touched there is bliss
A heaven with no aperation
A call like the rise of a nation
So tender and pure
The heart is unsure
A twinkle so open is vast like the ocean
Low tide reveals the love that we hide

Journey to the East

Rebirth for love
Reunited with true self
No longer poor in spirit
I had eternal wealth
Reawakened heart
An inner glow
Releases a natural flow
Our souls to mate
Remembered memories run parallel
A journey far
To relight me
I lost what I needed
Becoming receded
For a precious moment
She revealed the love in me

Hidden

Internal combustion
Prolongs the interlude
A yearly minute opens the spirit
Enter the light for inner peace
The realm of the deceased
A message dark
A recovery hour
Returns lost power

Taken

A phantom unnoticed
Waiting for the moment
Silence or sleep
Slowly you creep
Holding people for ransom
While uplifting their ransom
I condemn thee to ill health
Why me I have little wealth
I remain in paranoia
Ever watchful for the phantoms stealth

Daily commute

A daily view both near and far
Awash with emotion a yearly commotion
A sea of upturned smiles
Comfort defiled
Repetition is an updated edition
Enforced is our journey
We travel with haste
Disembarked into a land of waste
Barely able to gaze at another man's face
Footsteps of the damned
Though separated we walk hand in hand
Hypnotic the rhythm as we face indecision
Our hearts sorrowed by the incision
A way of life so cruel

Playful Thoughts

Inside is spiritual
Outside need a miracle
Internal remains
External barren terrain
Superior the lesson
Inferior the thought
Anterior is sought
Posterior we are caught
Above is our wish
Below we have missed
Abducted society
Adducted reality
Fast is the pace
Slow is the disgrace
Anger is the position
Happiness true religion
Left is the demand
The right path leads to a new land
Medial for trust
Distal brings distrust
From the top is spiritual
At the bottom need a miracle

Rebirth

The world is not for me
Through a mirror
Life feels anew
A mother exorcises her baby from a demonic cry
We live as was meant to be
A day is not a survival
I am and that is free
Not watched or having to perform
In this existence golden age cannot be formed
No longer tribal the mind has the faculty to be reborn

Memories

I replay to remember
A gift of joy that also brings sorrow
We as humans wonder so much
It seems so close to feel the dream
Sensual sensors awaken the touch
Am I here or over there
Can I revert the hands of time
Remember good times and become encased
Is this reality
I can remain in this wondrous place
Why not it feels sane to remain
Refrain the present
Future can recall
The past is mine until I fall

Prostitution

I reached a low and resorted to the oldest profession
Prostitution
Tired of society and eternally searching for a solution
I was young of mind
Ready to quit
This new life seemed so fine
Work comes fast
No strenuous interview all it takes is a quick view
Soft skin and still supple
To all new clients I am the divine
Shy and coy not used to grand places
They touch me I never remember their faces
I feel in my heart I need and choose to receive
When in demand I spark for attention
Then comes the shock when my services are through
Back to what
I forgot I existed
Money and fake pleasure for being a part of their leisure
I was so amazed
I have finally come of age
They offered me a world of dreams
The ride was easy and for a moment happy
And this became my perpetual drug
Whatever they say and wanted me to do
I learned fast to follow these rules
They came at me with smiles to light the way
I had nothing so there was little I could say
Belittling myself by presenting a gift
A friend told me I was on a beginning to the end that day
Staying with my kind made things real
The reality came as I came home embedded with pain
I complained and they came down on me with no restrain
Leave I must this life has no trust
I was shocked by their distrust
They told me a truth
Young I maybe but dark skin sells little
They know my clients on my own I would fall
Suddenly things seemed so small
Is this all I am cash in their hands
Trying a new life my past cannot be revealed
They know and wait for me to return in confusion
How could I fall under their simple illusion
Poverty makes self-esteem fall into a well
Let me seek another, surely I would not get the same bother

Life comes full circle when you act a fool
My client called as they wanted me back
Due to my mistrust they played tricks to stab me in the back
What I am to do as I get older
With jealous eyes I look at new youth with despise
Failing to realise they are a reflection of me
They call knowing I have no where to go
To hell with them
Though fallen like snow I wait alone to plant a new seed and hope for it to grow

Pressure Performance

On the Astral field from above
I gaze with a stare mimicked across the boundary
Written is perfection
The lost in spoken is contrite
Surreal environment supposed to entice
Judgement on my pose
My performance relies on verbal prose
Can there not be a better way to test

New generation

The fortitude of youth
We lie uncouth
Seeking to prevail is our holy grail

Remember me

Do you know who I am
Laid to rest is the forgotten man
Attention that most sought word
One day like any other
There is no cover
Transparent without mention
I holler to no avail
As they hammer another nail
This crucifixion leads to my sad diction
To disappear
Will anyone interfere

My Smile

I can't smile anymore
I look around waiting for the sound
True nature surrounds a moment for bliss
I still look around waiting for a sound
I can't smile anymore
A story told in prism reveals the same omega
Striving through this saga realising we have yet to reach potential
I can't smile anymore
Repetitive strain
Daily repetition
I seek a new high where is the astral plane
Same faces seeking new places
I can't smile anymore
Where is the respect
They cannot see regret
Attain for what
Look for meaning when permanently forgot
I can't smile anymore
God save me
Spirit cleanse me
Split faces reside on holy ground
Commandments of choice
Do we really listen to the voice
I can't smile anymore
Look for happiness
Look for wealth
Look of love
We look below continue a search where there is nowhere to go
I can't smile anymore
They are better
She is fatter
Oh you really care and ask what is the matter
I can afford
Yet still we are bored
Seek the umbilical cord
We don't really smile anymore

Customs

The age of check in
What do we bring today
Past or future
So scared of lost we would rather refrain from leaving the ground
A look inside reveals
Yet we still carry on
Places are people what we bring is not new
Reacting from memories
The feeling remains in a whisper
The years unfold to increase our load
Yet when we check out the return is unwanted
The truth is delayed in the luggage we brought

My Town

This is my town
I believe I own it
It owns me yet apart
I can be free
I know him and her
I remember sitting by the tree
I can tell you how the wind blows
Or when last that it snowed
The shortcut to the station
The neighbours that I miss
Which is the best chippie
And the streets you should miss
My town was silent an echo brings alert
It has been not five years
When I return I feel hurt
Where are the trees
Expansion all around
Who are these people
No one remembers my name
Look in the sky and all I see is a crane
No land is safe no space is free
Brick after brick
My town what have they done to it
The air feels different my shortcuts are blocked
Most shops are closed
New families casts lots
To obtain a sought after spot
The shops are revamped the prices too steep
Have to be careful on all streets as danger tends to creep
What language is spoken
Can hardly hear myself think
Look around and kids mainly drink
This is too much I feel out of touch
My town is no more
Oh look they want to build another superstore

Shimmer

I am replaceable as a glass vase
If it shatters would it matter
A look at the reflection
Casts a shadow
Hollow is the sound
Glass is not unique
New shapes and colours the identity remains weak
Recycled once broken
Fragile glass remains forgotten

The Boy

Free as a boy playing by a well
Danger and excitement to him it is joy
No fear the entrapment of risk
Weighs not on his mind
Tomorrow is today
He lives simple no pausing
The cause of decision is not precise like a medical incision
Full of creativity often dismissed as a wild child
He laughs at adults afraid once they step outside
What mysteries can he tell
Let us look inside the well
A velocity transponds
The young boy did fell
What of life can past by
As he surely will die
Does he have regret or follow the ride
Young in spirit
He rejoices to live then to die

Heal

Magical circumference embedded in my finger
Energy waves vibrate
From the earth and universe
To heal and return to the dirt
Dance and rhythm to restore the inner flame
Take my power
How can I conduct without a choir
Yet the vibrations still lead a healing song
The mystery of the oil from a flower
Synergy for empathy
Restore the good memory

Seeking the truth

What is it all about
Life is an illusion or do we travel in vain confused by the conclusion
I used to think I could steer clear of the system
Not conform to ensure I was really born
Eventually the daily assurance negates negativity
The positive that I know what is around
What is my worth is this the earth
A hole in the ground reforms to make new land
The mystery it will always be yet for eternity
To open ones mind restore prehistoric time
What or where is the divinity

What can you see

We mainly realize it when were alone with it
Everyday it remains atmospheric
Easily forgotten
It naturally rises
Serendipity to appreciate often is too late
When it falls down
Do we look to help it
Continue on and so it continues
It needs no support yet appears for us to gaze
We are blinded in the maze of our opportunity
What a task in our lives to panoramically focus

The Quest

I went down this morning
What did I see looks like there is nothing for me
Do I really have to watch TV
Its tricks play the jealous game with me
When I step out there is none around
Yet there is always plenty of sound
Speak to the pimps have they anything for me
Oh that game
I see
Back to the place
Where nothing arrives unless I have commodity
A symbol that rules all
Without we all fall
Without it I disappear
Without it nothing to do
If you think you can live without then you know not the rules
Well what can I do

The urge

I like sex so much that I am fucked
Can I help it, is it simply a part of my make up
Explosions of testosterone
Look at someone and visualize them groan
Every second every hour
To me they are all flowers
Or should that be flour
I add ingredients for me to mould
Is it wrong
Am I right
My perception
Elicit thoughts at night
A constant journey for moments of pleasure
I endeavour and I devour every flower
Nature forsaken to hear the peak of a sound
Is it really progressing the species or increasing disease
Of the mind let alone the physical
The greatest weakness to rule mankind
Is there love or only sex
Do we know
Psychic mind what is next
So un-complex is the beauty
Forever more the world is on a sexual tour

The Rainbow that frees

A rainbow people think is fantasy
It exists
Where I go to indulge in fantasy
I know it is false
The reason I am here for some paid affection
Erected thoughts
They know my heart so in their web I am caught
Hypnotic is the vibe
In here we are all alive
Sense of belonging
United purpose
In trance raising spirits by dance
There is something youthful almost freeing
For one night I increase my well being
We gather
Bathed by the lather
Your false looks easily hook
I cannot touch yet still feel
A surreal dream
When I leave I hide afraid to be seen
Some will be disgusted
For what shame
Inside I am free feeding false joy
Men like their toys and ladies know to
A rainbow is sought to make dreams come true

Time to wake up from the dream

A pattern like a puzzle can be tackled in many ways
If we each enter a maze
The goal is a shared destination
We seek anew when it is only a change in yesterday's repetition
Cursing life without realising our confusion
Our patience remains brief as like a child
Adventure we seek often afraid for fear makes us weak
So we conform leading an illusion called the norm

Visual Mirror

I want the woman in a picture
The one who stays close
Someone I can adore
Who listens with me
Never leaves or tries to deceive
Her vision astounds our moments stay precious
Her life is for us others come second
Nothing I say brings a strain
If lost on a plane our hearts would find each other
Connected like a homing beacon
To feel totally at ease with no need to appease
I remain me and she is a picture
Each day brings a memory
I can reach out and be transfixed by the trust forever
Unified we live in our own special reality

Generation Zero

What are you looking at
Paranoid schizophrenic delusion
You want to play gangster then be a zero
A superior mind rarely helps at this time
Are you troubled
Are you bored
Ready to attack because you can't afford
Accumulation of material is immaterial
Lack of foundations has ruined this young man
I understand living as if damned
Apathetic sounds to close to being pathetic
Can you sleep at night knowing tomorrow may be a final day
You give a shit
Well manure can bring a cure
What I am looking at the failure of society
Generation zero lost seeking a hero

Finished

A sense to quit brings forth the shadow of death
Relinquishes the soul forever more
The commitment to soar remains grounded
On uneven ground a growing fester
Awaiting change to loosen the cage of the torment
Believing that one is truly finished

The Ultimate release

True calm is the sensation of a flick with the palm
Releasing energy universal

Lone Wolf

I rely on myself as a lone wolf
Pleasure of my company
Who can understand accept self
Born alone
Raised to pass these trials
I deny reliance for it weakens the soul
To truly awaken requires ultimate self control
Placing others ahead means I stay backwards
Patrolling shadows
Adaptation for what lies ahead
Instincts enhance to circumvent the game of chance
Cosmic survival
Led to denial
Centuries of pain
Age of independence
Selfish lone wolf starts a revolution to restart prehistoric evolution

To care

Three dimensional care is the only way for spiritual consideration
Anything less causes denial
The direction the right path
Be humble though fortune may crumble
Empathic scheme is not a plan
Listen and understand
Lack of merit returns blessed grace
We care
Do we know how
In a dimension affinity is not bound
So we should inspire to reach a higher plane of thought
Rather than to rely on the morals we are taught
To care far beyond and accept things to be gone
To be deemed alternate and tragically go on
You have shown the true meaning of the word care

Troubled Soul forever seeking

To see what you have missed for most of your life
I witness beauty and thank fate for being so kind
A cycle of loving thoughts enter the mind
Though I often feel scared
With worries and fear
I thank someone that you are here
My heart reaches out often confusion comes from the mouth
Though we never met we have our special dance
Entranced by the energy that realised my inner glow
Surprised by my words often truly felt
When you feel near the earth falls from under
I wonder about
Dismayed without you I long to touch you
Others may try to steal you away
I know my sweet that I shall have my day
The world will stop the heavens be open
I have waited so long with such devotion
Awaiting the hour when we both see the same stars
A perfect moment
Feel our pleasure
Let us float to sky and yonder on high
As a bird feels free when we meet you can unravel me
With patience
With my usual fear
I await you dear

Fast Women

Fast women
Your movement is untrue
Entice
Do represent all things nice
A female form shaped to perfection
Subconsciously and automatically
Your vision rules
Hypnotic
Tricking men as our thoughts turn quick to erotic
Romance has not a chance
We camber in packs to ask for a dance
Casting money for you be a wishing well
You know the game
You know we look
Manipulating our simple psyche does not let us of the hook
The chase continues into future times
Fast women move too quick for eyes to see
Blinded by what I believe you can offer me
Slowing down I visualize a glimmer of your distortion
Quite twisted
Though I still remain eternally addicted

Lets be free

Soften heart with nardostachys jatamansi
It must flow free as sand
For harden sand does not make a foundation for land
We cry out when there is no need for desertion
Wandering to reflect in wonder
Disease can be conquered if we are true
To be complete resist from seeing in the distance
Enrapture your realisation
Devotion to spirit wild water becomes still
The thrill, exuberance the second dimension releases your will

The fear of love

Does the world understand love or is it simply looking above
Tell me what do you see a void in our souls
We journey not knowing where to go
Listen
Why listen to what others say
Are they going my way
Never
Why do we bother to exist like this
When the point of life is missed
Our thoughts eclipse revelation
Can mankind reveal salvation or go forth into damnation
Commercials saying I am lost
The humiliation is done so I pay a cost
Working lives where we struggle to survive
Pretending we are alive
Inside we have died living a lie
Stop and look at weekends desperation of an entire generation
Born in a fluxed conception on the streets with no discretion
Well it has been played in many songs on TV everyday
Books and once a year in a shop window display
We know but keep it forgotten
Something must be wrong
When the answer has been said
Yet still we struggle with thoughts tormenting us in bed
Superego for the living dead
Remember in the beginning what I said
Does the world understand love
Is it looking for intervention
Why are we so afraid to love again

Be as a child

Spiritual, political and religious collisions
Can be ended by innocently embracing acceptance like a child

The Meaning of Indecision

Unaware of future tense
The predicament of a moments decision
Guidance is forked like lines in hand
One single second
Destiny a month a year or century
So cruel this faculty
Does it hinder me
Is this a play for He
Everything must have a reason
There is no such thing as indecision

Watched

To peek out with a cry of freedom
Innocently approaching in the distance what lies
Survival is nature's key word
Blundering forward I seek who observes
A lone shadow cast brings attention
Startled and surprised surrounded by their eyes
The heart quickens
Adrenaline for intervention
Speed of feet to save me from defeat
I cower a shelter for me to hide
Human nature so much to realise

Dark night kiss

The mystery of evil
What a life it implores
Deception of reality with instant ramification
Look towards it with no condemnation
A price to pay
Devoured with little delay
Can you touch it to magnify your power
Cometh the storm prepare for an eternal hour
It never searches for it is often found
They say the world has laid down
Enchanting its kiss to reverse our thoughts
The good are weak a fight easily fought
Forever we must resist a touch of infection
To come close to our resurrection

A world needing answers

Harshness hardens the heart
Threats make us a timid
Insults leave us conflicted
Pain breeds us to be vindictive
Rejection a need for approval
Anger feeds us with raw power
Spite has someone to blame
Fear the wonder should we be here
Hatred the cause to ignorant
Loneliness living indifferent
Unloved seeking for care
Violence a feeling of despair
Criticism a lack of wisdom
Jealousy believing we are better
Terror thinking it may last forever

Conditioned

Like demons cast out of souls we are scattered into
the night left with are own misfortune
No longer can we behold
The fortitude of existence mystifies indefinitely
Seeking solitude in body when the truth is spirit
Captured by the physical
The mind justifies this terrain
Higher planes obstructed by a new day
We plan to increase constriction
Narrowing our thought
Pure magic is from where we came
Chaos circle rides to take us back
We create war when our conditioning needs to be attacked

Physic Empathy

We have this power to go further than the present
Watching through my many points of view
I touch to reveal
Mentally renewed
Physic empathy the begin of the faculty path
One look
You are naked
Not undressed if you sense this then you remain clothed
We are part of a collective but seek to remain independent
The original source remains in our genes
Therefore our life is yoga
Empathic should be our state of nature
Left not just for mothers
Our will is an embryo
For us to grow we need to realise our true stature
Return to the divine in life collectively
Seek and see the third eye
Our purpose
Our faculty

All I can give is love

All I can give is love
Who do you seek
Yourself
Or the comfort of wealth
No desire to be alone
A basis to be grown
Sexual
Spiritual
Self critical you push back
When you have a chance to create a home
All I can give is love
Why wonder why
Independence
Separation
You keep looking when you have already died
We dream
Embrace rapture
A simple love gives me laughter
All I can give is love
Why not return it
No need to hide from it
You deny
Living life pretending not to cry
Are you happy
Cannot feel happiness
Do you want happiness
Confuse
Complex
You move from one to the next
Simply sex
Actually you deny
What is perfect
No universal definition
Let us nurture
Come hold my hand
Where to begin
All I can give is love

Flower on the Wall

Flower on the Wall
What is your story
I can guess
Blessed be by thy name
Holy is the ground
What has fallen
What is left
Only a flower
That fades with every coming hour
Life walks by
The flower dies
Symbolic is the sight
For those connected it brings fright
Flower on the wall
You bring meaning
A chance for reflection
A beauty that dies
This is nature
To gaze upon you makes me cry

Repent

Can you forgive
Not me
I mean you
What have you done to be so low
Are you so bad you need a life sentence
When I look at you should you turn away
When I give love
Does it bring life or decay
Hollow your soul
The echo is your own condemnation
How can you live
How can you love
When you torture yourself as if rejected by God above

I Believe

I believe
People are wary of religion
I believe
A path is set no matter wrong decisions
I believe
The past can stop future repetition
I believe
There is love inside you
I believe
Good can come from disaster
I believe
Strength can make my dreams come true
I believe
I am good as I am
I believe
A light will shine through
I believe
Because someone has to
I believe
For life to revolve
I believe
To reset fate
I believe
As I am my own master
I believe
To survive
I believe
I am alive

Slave Master

Why chase the master
Because in his status he will fall
Enslaved I maybe
But life to death the human soul will always be free
My spirit though down
Awakens
In reality the master is his own slave
And I am truly awakened
To conquer is to find a bigger place to hide
The fear inside only brings you closer to judgment
My master my slave
What lies beneath the grave

My Prayer

Dear Lord from my heart an open prayer
I understand not fully
Please grant upon me wisdom
Help me when others remove the ground from under me
I try to be the son to listen to his Father
Am I forever weak or simply disobedient
Many my wrongs
Why do you continue to bless me
Hopefully my heart is satisfied with love from You
I see so much wonder
Miracles and nature
Blessed Father am I worthy of You

The first touch

Time stands still
Stars come out at daylight
For a moment I have a vision
Homeostasis flows through the body
A glow divine
I am now weakened
Yet I endure marvelled on this magical tour
A tour where my eyes cannot be opened
I can feel visualization
When released
I have found peace

Death touch

Embraced by death the world had fallen
Nothing around
Tears bringing thunder the ground
Pierced with precision by the samurai's blade
Inscriptions appearing on an unknown grave
Temporal disfigurement relives moments that brings a wish
A second chance for negativity to be dismissed
Death has a power to bring life to the living dead
Rebirth from the pit dissolution
Arise now is not the time to die

Birth

You can never lose that part of you
Our hearts were beating as one
You nourished me made a home for me
When I gazed upon you I cried
For a moment I needed to return inside
Bringing comfort
So much to teach
Longing for speech
You make me stand tall even when I fall
Our lives together
Eternal connection
That cannot be broken even in separation
Not just for set backs
You are my inspiration
Through my creation
Though I fail often to show it
You are my devotion

www.ingramcontent.com/pod-product-compliance
Ingram Content Group UK Ltd.
Pitfield, Milton Keynes, MK11 3LW, UK
UKHW041433180426
11947UKWH00007B/413